Gallery Books
Editor: Peter Fallon

WHALE ON THE LINE

Nuala Archer

Whale on the Line

 Gallery Books

Whale on the Line
is first published
simultaneously in paperback
and in a clothbound edition
In July 1981.

The Gallery Press
19 Oakdown Road,
Dublin 14
Ireland.

Cover design by Michael Kane

ISBN 0 904011 21 6 (clothbound)
      0 904011 22 4 (paperback)

 The Irish Distillers/Patrick Kavanagh Award is awarded annually
to an Irish poet in respect of a collection of unpublished work
judged superior to the others received. The judges in 1980 were
Peter Fallon, David Marcus and Catherine Slattery.
Acknowledgements are due to the editors of *Another Chicago Magazine, Blue
Unicorn, The Carlton Miscellany* (Minnesota), *Creme City Review* (Wisconsin),
Cyphers, Davidson Miscellany, Epoch, The Gorey Detail, Impact (California),
New Irish Writing (The Irish Press), *Poem, Salomé* (Chicago), *The Stony Thursday
Book, Stylus* (Illinois) and *Windless Orchard* (California) where some of these
poems, in whole or in part, have been published.

The Gallery Press gratefully acknowledges the assistance of An
Chomhairle Ealaíon (The Arts Council of Ireland) and Irish
Distillers in the publication of this book.

Contents

*to Anne Archer, Bob Siegel,
Dawn Webber, Pam Ore
and Ken Pobo*

Burial

An ox is patiently plowing
me into the ground. A worker
par excellence, carefully broken in,
is it a basket of starry grapes
that lures her or a laser goad?

Day and night I hear her hooves
above me slowly plodding
the black furrows washed pink
with the setting sun, dyed
yellow in the morning.

She lumbers toward the red
calligraphy as if it were a door
or a trough of mint barley water.
She casts a barrel silhouette
and snorts the air's soft bones.

While everybody sleeps
and branches lace the moon's belly
the ox plows on balancing
silver coins of night
like egrets or drops of dew.

In the morning she shakes night off
and plows it in over my head.
I am driven deeper and deeper
into darkness. The ox continues
plowing. She plows through fields

of Greece and Rome. She plows
copper rain and blue snow into
the ground. She plows pinwheels
of children, cows
and hay-filled barns into the ground.

Her muddy feet spell a mosaic
of disappearance. The infinite black
box glitters under her.
She plots the release of Persephone
and listens to wind publishing her marrow.

Hunting the Sloth

You'll find her curled in trees
dangling like over-ripe fruit,
this most tenacious burr

with a power to resist that impresses
the most conscientious Quaker.
Her defence is a joke:

suspended invisibility.
Plants blossom on her
years before her funeral.

Don't look for a nest of foliage.
The sloth eats leaves until nothing
but air surrounds her. She is

a singing ventriloquist. Her pennywhistle
sound is heard only at night.
Don't trust the tone to guide you.

The Wedding Day

1.

On the run through the North woods,
through parallels of curling birch
and pines dark as guns,
crashing over ice plates,
over the brink of clouds,

the albino
deer dreams of snow
pulsing in black hooves.
She is the pause, the interval

between bank and break.
Padding his approach
the hunter mirrors sleep.
This is his wedding day.

2.

Hooves, like musical notes,
clip pitches of blue,
climb higher and higher,
print the earth—

past the trance of tree
after tree, past retreating ants
and brittle wasps, lightened
pumpkin patches, caterpillars
in a criss-cross of threads.
Past the cicada nymph
slumbering toward sunshine,

the albino hurdles the hardened
vertebrae of the river.

3.
The hunter
is a harmony waiting in the mesh
of grass. He is the impelling shadow
full of love for the bounding albino.

4.
After the bow of stars,
the occult of red fur,
paralysis throngs the eye,
triggering a flurry of leaves.

Snowbound

1.
White fills all space.
There is no room to move.
We are water-tight.

Molded where we are
snow creates new levels
over us.

It packs us into ourselves.
We become solid and
one.

2.
I look out my window.
The road is gone.
The trees, with exchanges of colours and birds,
are gone.

There are no neighbours
shovelling shadows out of ice,
sentencing breath to the moon.
There is no moon. No sun. No sky.
No spinning wheels.

Everywhere
everything
is mortared
into the stonework of snow.

3.
When we could go for walks
we heard snow
and gave it form.
We laughed and said
God's teeth are falling out.
We knew we had blood.
Snow turned us red.

Now, locked inside,
we are whiter than sunlight.

Sailors

Snow melts to make us sailors.
Our houses float free and knock
against each other like sampans.

Suddenly, we are alone,
the direct object of the sea,
surrounded by waves—black

to blue to peacock green—
capped with metallic shimmer
like saws cutting toward us.

Our thoughts, possessed
by the green delirium, disappear.
Nothing changes here.

The roll and tumble
drowns articulation.
Water is inhumanely sincere.

Absorbed by the horizon
we are one knot
liquefied in the ravellings

of the anchorless sea.
With the staring eyes of Queen Hatshepsut
who sent the earliest crew

over this morgue,
we pick a direction from the stars.
We ask Bright Dog and Great Bear

to throw us fire.
Nothing leaves tracks for us to follow.
We watch the planets grow.

A mullet moon and plover sun
reveal our corners
to the cannibal tides.

Whales rub their bulk
against our windows.
Barnacles attach to riggings.

Our hair is stiff with salt
and the smell of seaweed.
There is no harbour from the storm—

a quarrel of flashing knives
in the sky, splintering
the stained glass sea,

reassembling us in another dimension,
cloaked with scales
and the fine white muslin of fog.

Whale on the Line

for John

1.
You can't hear me dialling your number
because a whale is tangled
in the telephone cables on the ocean floor.
For some unknown reason

he torpedoed to the bottom. Cables entwine
the spool of his body—forty-five tons
of blubber the colour of your blue eyes.
His last air bubbles drift up

like small parachutes. He explores
the darkness by ear, listens
to kelp wave solemnly back and forth
like ushers at a funeral.

It took the scuba divers
days of overtime to unknot the mesh.
Arc lamps scattered light
in strange shadows. A white octopus

floated about, curling and uncurling
his arms like yo-yo's, gently touching
the whale's slack muscles,
open mouth and lidded eyes.

2.
For months words drift in shoals
around the quiet whale . . . 'Remember
nightingales, stars, hibiscus, the late
train, willows of wind . . .?'

Fish gargoyles, carrying lamps,
pick barnacles off the whale's back.
Submarine gulls circle and scream
Ballena! Ballena! Kujira! Kujira!

The whale's skull lies in sand.
A seaweed tongue flutters with the tide.
His stoney ears patiently become
the water sounding against a calf

just born to blue-green September
light. Soft explosions of breath
buoy her thermos-shaped body.
An albatross wraps the five-foot cord

around its neck, tears into placenta
as a clean wind tears clouds open.
Half-awake the calf rolls with the slanting
sea into a night brightened by the moon's

rainbow witches. Fog horns call back memories
of ships—*Union, Essex, Ann Alexander*
and *Kathleen*—sent to the bottom by whales;
and of whales lashed to my call of love for you.

Christmas in Dublin

It is the cat within us—
roosting, eyes half-closed,
on the central heating vents
above the heart—
which holds us in Keegans'
where turkeys and ducks droop
from the ceiling.
It is this cat which wonders
at the power
that brings the speed
of these birds to zero.

While we buy cranberries,
leeks and lettuce
and joke about the gamey
smell nuzzling into our wools
and moulting hair, the cat
is rivetted to claws
tied to S-shaped hooks.
She sees the taut bodies
and bills pointing
like arrows through floorboards.
She knows the kill is not
complete until her teeth
touch the wishbone.

The cat
is calculating Christmas
dinner. This is the sparrows'
chance to possess the garden
and the juniper's fallen berries,
to dance on the window-ledge
in the peat fire's reflection
and to gather the guarded crumbs.

Your Philodendron, a Frightening Heart, Discusses our Relationship

I once was you
spinning the alphabet's roulette
wheel into bloom
until a field of poppies

floated above me.
Scrabbled by rain and roots
I spelled this green plant
growing beside you

like elephant-ears, tiger prints
or a frightening heart.
We share this study,
this February night,

breathing each other
in and out.
The desk lamp spreads
a net of light

across your coral brain
and the map of my leaves.
You suspend words like high wires
for ants balancing burdens.

I release shadows
and throw them across cordons
of books, walls and bed.
Even you are a screen.

These monster murals are the real
home movies. While you
recall Mother
I remember the widow
I am.

These Sumac Branches, My Prison

1.
Brick walls are hell
to compose. I watch
light jig the rectangles.
Sparrows rappel the face.
It frustrates me,
the wall staring
bullish and bloodshot.

Now I have a tree. I am
zebra-striped with shadows.
These dark ribs won't wash off.

2.
I sleep on a bed that springs
from a closet of coat-hangers.
The intangible highways
of the tree still run
across my stomach and hands.

Swaying limbs incorporate
my arms and legs into
a windy rumba. Leaves
web my face, float
through my neck,
carouse in hips and calves.

3.
I drift awake
and cannot distinguish
between leaves and moths.

If I could step outside
my skin I would climb
the ladder of light tossed
against my trunk.

The bed is a loom
of shadows. I am
woven into a tissue
of wings—butterflies
buckling a tune.
A torn moth is stuck
in my yawning eye.

4.
This is my 8,118th day
in the hubbub of foliage.
Drifting moments stitch
together New York, Canada,
Costa Rica, Ecuador, Panama,
Texas, Chicago, Milwaukee and Ireland.

Leaves button me to the moon.

The Blues

sweep through
like a death angel
as monkeys pass
each enclosed hour
searching for ticks
boring into the blood
like flaming eyes.

Eyes between every hair,
eyes under the tail,
eyes on necks and backs,
eyes between fingers,
crawling up stomachs.

Every pore is bloodshot
shining like a ruby,
crossed with bars
and iron shadows.

Possessed,
the monkeys
silently rave
meticulously
hunting for eyes.
They crack each eye
they find,
chew it slowly,
carefully.

They don't want
these eyes
to set up
an internal business.

Passing By

Perhaps you are a child again, walking
in the woods at Coole, knowing more
than ever now that the stable door
isn't locked though the key is placed
with great ceremony on grandfather's palm.

Nobody would tell you how the calf
had come and so you waited up—
watching the dark ground,
wondering how a baby could dig
his way through so much earth.

There aren't even roses to mark
the place where you lie—just slugs
clinging to the side of grey stone
and rat holes connecting
your dreams with the centuries' dead.

Building a Sanctuary

1.
Stuffed with clouds
this crane is a question mark
balanced on one foot
in a museum's glass case.
Beside her
a brown and buff Labrador duck,
an unappealing condor,
two heath hens
frozen in a sociable chat,
a great auk,
cheerful Carolina parakeets
and *Martha*
the last of her species,
a passenger pigeon
who died at 1 p.m.
September 1, 1914,
aged 29.

2.
People think I'm crazy
building a sanctuary,
stocking it full of blue crabs,
lacing a crescent coastline
with mudflats and lagoons,
covering shores with sand,
blackjack oaks and sweetbay brush.
They don't know whooping cranes are melting
like snow from the earth.

3.
I listen on riverbanks
for the wingbeat.
The wind sifts
a faint trumpeting vocabulary.
Friends tell me not to worry.
They give first-hand reports
of great flocks
but I only see
plumes of sunlit cloud,
cowboys in Cessna broncos and
wildcat oil wells catching fire,
dappling the sky with ash.

4.
In autumn
the first pair arrives.
They spend months in marine meadows.
As spring softens the ground
the birds begin to dance—
leaping into air
bills pointed skyward.

Each runs toward the other
bowing
flapping bright wings
sliding over scrub
slowly gaining elevation.

Their shadows float
on my forehead
as they move toward the music
of eggs, like whole notes,
breaking open.

Re-acquaintance with Lumbricus Terrestris

Today, on my way to the library
I was interrupted by a small movement.
An immature earthworm humped and sidled
its ringed cord of brownish-red

across the sidewalk's white expanse.
I blinked with impatience. What a strip
of stupidity—one of nature's loose ends!
I crouched to see the featureless face.

'You're a stupid jerk,' I whispered.
'An eyeless, earless, legless stupid jerk.
Get a heart and you'll stay underground.
Get some brains and you won't be

so inclined to chance the beaten track.
Your brothers are dried juice—
stains with no recorded history.
Why are you so engrossed in your own

angles, *LT*? And why do both ends
of your body explore opposite hunches
of vibration and light? Is your crawl
from some dark hole an impulse toward song?'

The Deviant Mantis

1.
Outside
the walnut-shaped foam tent
my wings yawn.

I watch siblings squeeze through,
honey-coloured,
dangling like animated bananas.

But not for long.
An excited shadow of ants
sends out hotlines,
hoards newborn gold.

2.
I'm alone on this leaf.
Massacre blurs memory.
Some sister or brother must be alive.
They are silent.

I call to the cricket.
He laughs at me,
keeps his distance,
says he does not want to chirp
in my stomach. Caves depress him.

Tomorrow there is a fiesta.
I want to dance
with a beautiful lady.
I want to kiss her green cheeks,
her supple neck and long gauzy wings.

The cicada hears me dreaming
and clashes cymbals in my face.

29

'We don't want priests
at our party. We want
to syncopate with nightingales.'

3.
The grass is black and brushes
me with dinosaur lashes.
Frog fever circles
the Milky Way.
Cuckoos whaleep, whaleep
while doodlebugs dig pyramids.

Yet I'm treated like a tiger.
Why is everyone surprised to see me?
Didn't my ancestors sing
or click to castanets?

4.
The single summer of life
is almost over.
I learned of my tradition
while losing my head.

One orange daybreak
in mid-October
my lady of dreams
swayed in sunlight.

I invited her to fiesta.
She extended her wings like a cross
and we flew into cathedrals
beneath chattering leaves.

While I embraced her
she nibbled off my head.
Such, I learned later,
is the custom.

I would have been
entirely hers.
Though decapitated
I stretched out my wings and feet
like blind men's canes.
I caught a branch
and pulled myself up.

Now I know why
the crickets and bumblebees
are afraid of me.

5.
I found I can function
without a brain. I have
other nerve centres.
Stories come to me
through my toes.
My wings are transparent antennae.

In China my relatives
are carried about in bamboo cages
and matched like fighting cocks.
In Japan they are tethered
to bedposts to catch mosquitoes.

I hear strange news
from all over the world.

Towards Another Terminal

Down silver eels
the train highballs
into the iron barn.
Its whistle moans
to the red-haired moon
as Ms. Fashoon sidles over
to Walter and a vodka gimlet.

Her eyes are strawberries
with green lashes.
She is a tall coyote
trying to bite her heart into
digestible pieces.
'Please,' she says,
'where's my man, where's the next
whistle blowing from, where
are my shoes in relation
to my head, will you be my
new earring?'

The train scribbles
a blackboard sky, its white
eye whips
the glittering rails
towards another terminal.

Eclipse

for Philip

The car blacked out
everything except itself.
Our blood customised the Maverick—

fuschia, cinnabar, violet.
Almost chrome ghosts, our stillness
reflected hubcaps and fenders.

People gathered round.
Their eyes pierced us like bullets.
We were Bonnie and Clyde—

solid steel; then, a mess of holes.
Cars pressed in
like black roses, black cats.

In glass and vinyl,
behind steering wheels
and speedometers at zero

old guys diagnosed
their lives by dashboard dials,
left light shafts boring into us.

Amid the honking and splutter
of revved-up engines,
we became the shadow of wheels.

Rocking

for Mary L.

These days I wake up crying
holding myself in my arms
rocking myself like a mother
repeating
it's all right—i'm here.
And the room I wake up in
rocks in the arms that are rocking
me. The walls move
like a sea ebbing and flowing.
They never rest and all the books
with their thousands of pages
and millons of words
which I can hardly read
move to the rhythm of
a hammock pushed by the indifferent
toe of a Cuna mother,
who is I, as she prods the
open fire and sings *nanas*
of sound which are not English
yet echo in my ear like
the surf in a shell.
The lamp on the desk and
all the pencils and the black,
golden-eyed kitten
looking at me—all move
to and fro with the room
swaying through space like
a pendulum that has swung into orbit,
spiralling now closer,
now farther away, and the
nails that fixed the room and me
to a place seem to be flying
in all directions

and I rock myself
and I rock myself
and the room rocks me
until I find my feet again
and can walk, learning to let go.

Staying

Wherever night overtakes her—
that's where she stays.
Yesterday, night overtook her
waiting for a train.
She stayed on the platform.
Tonight she is watching
a candle burn an eye into the moon.
Night takes her over.
She stays at the typewriter
migrating through the blackened keys.

Flaked Out on the Forbidden Grass at Chartres

for CJH and JNH

Look, they're sleeping—
father and son—
beauties—
carefully spaced out
on the grass, in the shadow
of flying buttresses
at Chartres.
Well, who isn't ready
for a cradle-song
after such boggling splendour
and then a picnic, to boot?

They're out beyond the count
of 10. Even at 1/2000
my camera can't click
the dream they're falling through.
Adam, pure smiling stone,
over by the North Door,
transfuses these relations
with possibilities. For instance,
while he rests his head
on his father's lap
his father gently contemplates
Adam's mop of hair.

This is the scene
twenty years after
Peggy
baffled the routine
of growing up
growing old—
out-stepped delay
and left these two men
sleeping—
each curled toward
his splintered skiff.

Riding Out a Storm

There is no need for a home.
When raindrops pound the earth
to dough and lash the hollyhock
back and forth through a great arc,

I cling to the underside
of leaves and wait for the typhoon
to whip itself still. I watch
clouds caricature ancestors—

such mounds the fluff makes
of them! And then the clouds
sift toward me like broken clocks,
like fragile ferries.

When every feather of water has
fallen from its perch, I am going
to climb some unheeding face and watch
eagles stress the teetering horizon.

Gypsy Asleep

This gypsy, dark
as a cacao tree, doesn't twitch.
She lies down before the blue door,
unsandalled, and smiles at the light

knocking through the moon-shaped
keyhole. Instead of a cuirass
she wears a rainbow. One could almost
mistake her for a wick compassed

by pinstripes of flame. A lion,
patrolling the copper sands,
bends over the sleeping gypsy

and hears birds whirring
in the chinks of her ears.

Dance of Wind and Wash

Unlike myself, there are women who do not lie
in bed every morning wondering: *Shall I get up?*
My mind roams capitals and anonymous
villages of the world and everywhere I see them
hanging out the most beautiful wash.

There is something about these women
and their lines of flowing shapes and colours
which prompts me from between sheets.
I get dressed and head north into where I am—
into the cold, clear light of the Pyrenees—
to photograph their laundry.

I pass hundreds of lines, each one distinct.
Some are taut and forthright, some relaxed
hung between trees or just outside windows.
The lines are their own horizons—
humming cables transmitting the glare of light.

Clothes are held to the lines by brown
or coloured pegs—bibs, bras and blouses,
blankets twisting into knots,
blue and pink striped sheets puffing
into spinnakers, nylons dancing, shoes hanging
disconsolately by their laces.

The sound of these threaded syllables swaying
like white shadows, a splayed deck of cards or arching
dolphins comforts me. I'm haunted
as much by the clothes as by bits of coastline
glimpsed between folds of bath towels.

I'm haunted too by your presence which hangs out
in my clothes, on my lines and whose ghostly
(and perhaps more substantial) swaying—
despite what seems a waste of lonely years—
I'm only now beginning to name.

Walking

We said goodbye to everybody
        and headed for anywhere
in the wilderness
            with muck and weeds
            and an absence of boundaries,
        to feel the planet
    under us
        rolling easily
        through the black eye of space.

After one hundred and seventy miles
        we are breathing again.
Blisters sprout on our feet
            like mushrooms. We lie
            in a field of sheep
        watching sun juggle
    light from tree to tree.
        Birds cluster like pine cones
        behind a cobweb.

It is no trouble
        to forget everything except
the hills and trees
            covered with lianas
            climbing like prayers
        and in the faces of sunflowers
    to see
            black buxom women
            telling of Red Horse River.

In the cold wind there is
        water-music—melting ladders
of snow surrounded
            by ferns, moss, milk-
            worts, goldenrods,
        briars and brambles.

Plants pull
    at our clothes to see
    what leaves unfurl from us.

Needing only the lean-to
    of our lonely selves we make
a bed of spruce
        branches and send squirrels,
        sunbeams and birds
    chasing after cracker
crumbs that stick
    in the sky
    like stars.

Mosquitoes, eating our arms and legs
        wake us
to another day
        of walking
        and pressing flowers
    into brain crannies.
We bring our sills
    to the very edge
    of a swamp

    to listen again
        to growing
thickets and lakefuls of lilies.